TWITTER
RESOURCE
BOOK

by
@jawar

1

TABLE OF CONTENTS

2009 JAWAR
ISBN 10 DIGIT:1508573255
ISBN 13 DIGIT:9781508573258
Library of Congress Control Number:

By @jawar

FIRST EDITION

Published by
P.O. Box 52682, Atlanta, GA 30355, USA
404-532-9324

www.jawarspeaks.com
Printed in the U.S.A.

Follow me @jawar or visit twitter.com/jawar

These folks help make this book possible with their quick THINK, PLAN, EXECUTE...

Book cover, one-sheet, flyer, business card, website design and hosting contact @judgemedia and @djjudgemental today! They designed the TWITTER SOURCE BOOK by @jawar

Tia Culver, Atlanta Publicist currently works with clients to increase their media profiles & gain exposure for their artist, product, service and/or event. Follow @tiaculver or 770-896-5685 tiacul@yahoo.com

Do you know what to do next to reach your goal? Create a system. Get details every Monday 9pm-10pm EDT on the live conference call 641-715-3620 CODE 1040565# Follow @coolwater101 socialsundays.blogspot.com

The purpose of this site this movement... is to motivate change, to aspire greatness and to showcase what you don't know because it's never talked about. Follow @hiphopgivesback Register at hiphopgivesback.org

If it were not for the Most High, my Ancestors, Family and Friends this would not have been possible. I'm eternally grateful!

This book was designed to be a directory of Twitter Tips, resources and applications to help the reader advance their knowledge on how to engage the community, share information and make some of the processes automated so you too may get more from your time. Because I put this book together in about 7 days there may be a number of errors throughout the book. If you can overlook this you'll find that this book is a powerful gateway to a wealth of resources and information that may dramatically transform your Twitter Activity within a relatively short time period. Keep in mind that while the information is extensive there's much more to be learned.

You may access more of this information by visiting the following sites:

www.jawarspeaks.com
www.twitter.com/jawar

The reader may also find they are in need of one-on-one consulting, should you be in this category you may contact me at @jawar or www.jawarspeaks.com

BIG SHOUT OUT TO
@judgemedia and @djjudgemental
for the awesome book cover design

TWEETS OF SUCCESS!

The tweets below were kept in original format, so you may read misspellings and what would appear as grammatical errors. However, bare in mind these are real people sharing feedback on their Twitter Experience.

 MizPecas @jawar I just wanted to let you know in the 3 week I've been following your advice I've gone from 121 follwers to 717. Thank you very much! about 4 hours ago from TwitterFon

 karenjonze new update on the blog entitled "Why am I single?" (inspired from a question by @jawar - thank you:D) http://bit.ly/wMFud about 8 hours ago from TweetDeck

 askodie LOVE TIP- Go give 'em a kiss right now and tell them "I love you!" (via @jawar)<--- he's right (Dude is an expert @ EVERYTHING!) about 10 hours ago from Tweetie

 cherlyn0217 @jawar thanks for the PRT @jawar you're very motivational! ;-)about 11 hours agofrom web about 11 hours ago from web

 STREETTALKCEO @jawar hey there jawar!! great seeing the actual you today.. i love your energy.. gave em a boost!!! about 19 hours ago from web

"Are you preparing for all the greatness that awaits you?"
JaWar

DanielleRicksWant to connect with creative business minds on Twitter? Follow @jawar @VincentHunt #Follow Friday
7:44 PM Aug 28th from web

Leslie84 @jawar i like your background it looks really good!!
6:53 PM Aug 28th from web

EvelynWellsMD RT @CBoogie1908: @jawar <----------- This man knows what he's saying!! #followfriday #motivation
6:43 PM Aug 28th from TweetDeck

HelloNorthGAHey @Jawar , you out there? Somebody plz find him...and when you do, #followfriday !5:23 PM Aug 28th from UberTwitter

Juicyfruit4uDriven,intelligent,inspirational,motivational speaker @jawar <==Make sure ur talking to him if ur serious about taking ur biz to next level 5:01 PM Aug 28th from TweetDeck

jchronowski47@jawar helps keep me motivated everyday in 140 or less #followfriday 2:47 PM Aug 28th from TweetDeck

MissPaulaFlavaRT @SlickTalkJ: Follow @jawar he's kinda a twitter guru.1:36 PM Aug 28th from UberTwitter

"Got enough marbles to play by myself, but that isn't fun so I'm sharing the wealth!" JaWar

 greggates RT @Janiro #FollowFriday @jawar thn gojawar.com and you'll c why! 1:24 PM Au28th from web

 ABCPublicity#FF @jawar he is constantly giving and has great life quotes that are in my FAVES!1:04 PM Aug 28th from web

 CBoogie1908 @jawar <----------- This man knows what he's saying!! #followfriday #motivation12:08 PM Aug 28th from UberTwitter

 sassieonduprisI met the homie @jawar for the first time in person and he a cool dude12:06 PM Aug 28th from web

 Wasi305slp#ff GreatMind/very informative/Great person 2 kno n follow @jawar<< Follow /learn/better you 11:42 AM Aug 28th from web

 ursulalr@MirrorFinish @jawar is an awesome recommendation to follow, thank you! 11:00 AM Aug 28th from TweetDeck

 DorethiaConner@jawar a man who will not teach you right won't treat you right? 11:00 AM Aug 28th from web

"Have a JAWAR Day -Be Happy, Healthy and Wealthy!"
JaWar

8

Miss_LeAnn@jawar no problem.. Thanks for the motivation and keeping me focused on my goals each day!.... #ff-----> @jawar
10:57 AM Aug 28th from UberTwitter

MirrorFinish Follow my friend @jawar who is one of the finest motivational speakers you will ever meet on Twitter.
10:56 AM Aug 28th from web

urbanperspectiv (Agree) rt @Nikki_Dreadz #FF U SHOULD BE FOLLOWING: @jawar: Motivational Speaker Empowers You to Power Yourse lf. http://jawarspeaks.com
10:25 AM Aug 28th from web

Fly11 RT @jawar: Motivational Speaker Empowers You to Power Yourself. Contact http://jawarspeaks.com<<<That Bwoy Good!
10:24 AM Aug 28th from TwitterFon

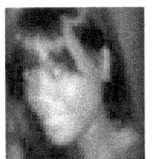
MDKayBee RT @MissPaulaFlava: #ff @princesstenia and @Mdkaybee both are so positive and affected me in a ^ way this week and I met them thru @jawar
10:23 AM Aug 28th from TweetDeck

jamesdickey I like @jawar He makes good points and has fun - an easy #followfriday recommendation 10:21 AM Aug 28th from web

TheMarketingMom @jawar #FF This man has paid his dues and is still paying them. A prime example of where you can get if you never stop pressing forward.
10:08 AM Aug 28th from web

9

reporter4651 #Follow Friday I'm a single parent & when I first joined twitter @jawar took time 2 offer me some good advice 2 help w/my son. Thanks Jawar!
10:01 AM Aug 28th from web

Persona_Affairs #FollowFriday --->@jawar = good people, good conversation and great connection! 9:36 AM Aug 28th from TweetDeck

ClintonSkakun #FollowFriday @jawar because he asks questions that could change the way you think about life.
9:31 AM Aug 28th from web

TferThomas *tips hat* Thank you sir! If you haven't met @Jawar then do so! RT @jawar PRT @TferThomas Pay it forward & share the love...#followfriday 9:16 AM Aug 28th from SocialScope

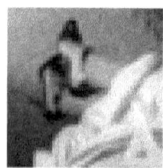

MizPecas @jawar #FollowFriday. His advice really works. He is what he says he is. The best thing on Twitter. His confidence is contagious.9:16 AM Aug 28th from TwitterFon

gatsbyiscrack Follow Friday eh? @ItsTangieBaby ...Sexy radio personality. @Jawar .. Some intellegent tips to motivate you in the right directions
7:45 AM Aug 28th from web

"Encourage your vision by taking immediate repetitive action."
JaWar

Ponchaveli_com When @jawarspeaks LISTEN! So Please follow @jawar! #FF
4:23 AM Aug 28th from web

gonzalocordova One with amazing words and such a heart!!! Connect to!! @jawar #FollowFriday (via @AliveinMe)
1:53 AM Aug 28th from Tweetie

AliveinMe One with amazing words and such a heart!!! Connect to!! @jawar #FollowFriday
1:50 AM Aug 28th from TweetDeck

dawnmitMany thanks to @jawar & @bodybychocolate for the great twitter tips! You guys are great!!!9:45 PM Aug 27th from web

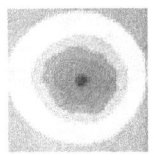

CoolAbstraction @Jawar I would pay for your motivational messages...I'm addicted to them now :) 9:33 AM Aug 27th from txt

TierraFilhiol Fantastic, your wisdom is my investment! RT @jawar: Yep, I'm still working. The new book is coming together.
10:14 PM Aug 26th from TweetDeck

vitality4all6 @jawar noticed PRT not only benefit the follower of mine but also benefits myself. Thank you.
3:11 AM Aug 26th from UberTwitter

"There's no way to sugar coat I love you, so just say I love you!" JaWar

11

 neuroaster RT @jawar ~ Start where you are and grow from there. #quote #jawar [This #aphorism is as concise as it is apt :)] #tweeght 3:05 PM Aug 25th from web

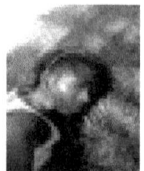 Dknlvlydiva @jawar thanks for being U.... Ur the best!!! Thanks for motivation, inspiration, networking, being a well rounded & informed individual ;) 2:20 PM Aug 25th from TwitterFon

 TheBentleyGroup @jawar @jaw I highly recommend checking out jawarspeaks.com It was like a Cup of RichCoffee We have to meet Good Morning America Break-Fast!

 kelvinringold @jawar You help a lot of people; just want to make sure the Universe has you in mind too ;) Enjoy your day. 8:18 AM Aug 25th from TweetDeck

 Stylescrybe @jawar you just got a mention on the 9000 Boys ustream show! Just thought I'd let ya know :-) 12:20 AM Aug 25th from twhirl

 JeTara #MrTweet I recommend @jawar because ... his tweets are inspirational and you can learn a lot from him. He can help you business wise! 6:18 PM Aug 24th from MrTweet

"I circumvent evil by doing good!" "Fear can cripple a dream or fuel ambition" "Love is the cure, true love has action behind it!" "Lift them up! I love this idea and the action behind it!" by @jawar

rickwilsonwmg @jawar I must say you are the networking king. I love the way you connect with people and I am taking notes.

Nana0507 @Jawar I sware he can lift anyone up from having a bad day...I haven't even seen a tweet from him yet but he was on my mind just that tough!

lyric7717 @jawar LOL, funny!!! I appreciate the motivational comments each day, just wanted u to know ur appreciated!!!

esdeereinvented @jawar Was just thinking how i need to stop trying so hard and be myself.. no idea how i found your tweet but it came just at the right time

K4S_Ent #SUCKAFREESUNDAYS @jawar this dude is inspirational. I read his advice and I feel more refreshed and focused to start the day

TriniChiniBarbi @jawar if it wasnt for u and ur quotes i wouldnt have made it through my day at work..so no thank u!

BrotherJesse If you are still looking for a speaker for your college campus, look no further than @jawar He will deliver!

msundertaker So now, I'm watching @jawar's videos with my boss so we can book him at our campus!!!

brittdeezy Need some inside info on the industry hit up @jawar or buy his book. Serious ppl only. He's the man 2 know!

BossLadiToya A SPECIAL THANKS goes out to @jawar and @jawarspeaks for the inspirational words and motivational quotes that you bring US. U R LOVED!

Bodyguard_Beats @jawar I need to take your Twitter seminar. I need more POSITIVE followers. Some ppl gripe 24/7. #getoverit Thx for PRT!

MBW_Productions @jawar How's it going sir! You've really helped me with marketing on here and in other areas, I appreciate you sir!

jayedii @jawar I love that statement among many others u post. U always have such inspirational quotes. I really enjoy following you!!

bigkenof334mobb @jawar <--follow the teacher.

Here are a few more people you'll want to visit and consider as each of them add to the Twitter Community in their own special way.

@tjsdjs –gave me the inside scoop on what's what
@unmarketing –one of my Twitter mentors
@tycohen –we host Motivational Music Radio
@sheriamore –it's perfect, riiiiiight
@bodybychocolate –we host Twitter Tip Thursdays
@insightpromos –super cool people, does marketing
@thediamondcoach –good person to know PERIOD!
@maestro –one of the coolest Grammy Winners ever!
@UCYIMD1 –well on the path the greatness.
@CBoogie1908 –vocal coach who has it going on.
@KayfromNJ –she's on the JAWAR RT Team
@dave_carpenter –we always exchange good tweets
@jshe –she's also on the JAWAR RT Team
@mylesmiller –he adds a positive tweet
@kprincess –always RTing and #mmradio family
@coolwater101 –has his own situation developing
@KevinGumbo –we go back like a teacher and student!
@ThriveAmerica -5 Business Motivators
@P10S –She's a writer who helps writers

If you didn't make this one no worries, it was the space not my heart!

TWITTER TIPS

TWITTER TIP- Add extreme value to your followers

This is by far one of the most important factors that can not be overstated. Many people often miss this point attempting to by-pass the social part of social media. Add value to your followers by sharing useful and practical information. Sharing a joke or two works well since most people enjoy laughing. With your jokes don't be to cynical or sarcastic. Sexist, racist and culturally insensitive jokes aren't good for business either. From time to time you'll want to share links with the community that may be of universal importance or current news. For instance, we may want to know if there was a huge earthquake in some part of the world or if someone launched a nuclear warhead. The point here is add value to the community, keeping in mind who your target audience is.

TWITTER TIP- Engage your followers-start conversations with people

When you want people to talk to you start talking first. Yes, this is by far one of the easiest things you can do on Twitter. Use Twitter to search a topic the same way you would search on Google. Because of the 140 character rule on Twitter I've found one to three word searches works best for me. As you search various words you'll want to start conversations with people you find interesting or have something of value to say. As your conversation continues you'll want to follow the people you engage. Typically, people will follow you once you follow them unless they are a mega celebrity with close to a million followers.

TWITTER TIP- Be yourself

It's good for your mind and spirit to be yourself anything else may make you a bit loony. Even the strictest of business professionals should share a bit of their personal side from time to time; it's what makes you appear human. Remember this is social media; it's not merely a place to promote and advertise, but to engage, share, learn and be an active participant. Be yourself in all the positive, encouraging and inspiring ways you know how. When I tweeted that I started running a mile a day or that I was going to swim with the dolphins many in the community seemed just as, if not more excited than I was. They were very curious as to why I would do those things, meaning what was the inspiration behind them. It showed that I was more than someone that sent motivational messages and quotes. Be yourself!

TWITTER TIP- Don't use DM so much it isn't picked up by the search engines.

DM means direct message and is Twitter's way of allowing you to send private messages. DM is good when you want to send a private message, but I've found you'll get more of the right followers when you have public conversations. Additionally, as long as your account's updates aren't blocked the search engines will pick up your Twitter Stream, thereby bringing you additional eyeballs and traffic.

When someone sends you a dm don't reply with a public tweet it may be viewed as rude, disrespectful and even incompetent. Keep in mind that both people have to be following each other to engage in a conversation using dm. If one isn't following the other the polite and professional thing to do is to send a public tweet to the other person saying "please follow me so I may send you a dm."

TWITTER TIP- Have meaningful conversations

Twitter is about engaging the community, having meaningful conversations and creating mutually beneficial opportunities from those conversations. As you add extreme value to the community, you'll find others doing the same. Remember in social media it's at least a two-way often multi-channel communication tool. With this in mind it's paramount to have conversations that will lead to being happy, healthy and wealthy for all parties involved.

TWITTER TIP- Go the extra mile to help others

Go the extra mile on Twitter. When one of your followers post a legitimate general question attempt to find the answer and respond back as soon as possible. Not only will you become the go to person in the community, but you'll learn a lot of information along the way. Go the extra mile to help others.

TWITTER TIP- RT messages you think are valuable to your followers (RT=retweet)

RT means to retweet. RT is like quoting someone on Twitter. If you are new to Twitter you'll have to copy and paste the person's tweet (message) and put RT in front of their name. RT is like saying you appreciate often approve of someone's tweet. RT is a simple way to get people's attention on Twitter. It shows the community you're not just about helping yourself, but helping others as well. Give and you'll get on Twitter. RT frequently.

TWITTER TIP- Give a lot; get a lot

The more you give solid, useful and practical information, motivational messages, quotes, jokes and resources the more you'll get in return on Twitter. By giving be a resource to the community, RT frequently and have a pleasing personality when tweeting. Give a lot and get a lot.

TWITTER TIP- Follow people who are in your niche market

This seems like a no-brainer, but follow people who are in your niche market even if they are so-called competitors.

TWITTER TIP- Don't follow everyone that follows you if you can't add vale to them or vice versa

This seems simple enough and it's true. Following the people that you can add value to and vice versa helps stay the task of networking with your target audience, colleagues and other business professionals associated within your industry or area of interest.

TWITTER TIP- Ask questions to keep your conversations going with followers

One of the easiest ways to get conversations started and get more followers is to ask questions. Keep in mind this was the premise for Twitter as the original question asked is "what are you doing?" Your industry, target audience, reason for being on Twitter and personality will determine what type of questions you ask.

TWITTER TIP- Include links every now and again when Tweeting to your followers

While 140 characters is a great way to stay concise it just isn't enough room all the time. Thankfully, you can include links were people may get details on a particular tweet, view a video and/or download a digital product or song. While you don't want every tweet to have a link, because it starts looking like spam it's acceptable to send a few tweets with links. Be mindful of your followers and target audience. Ensure that your tweets and links add value or people will begin unfollowing, ignoring and/or blocking your profile.

TWITTER TIP- Follow some of the big names on Twitter

Following some of the big names on Twitter is a good idea, especially when getting started. Following big names may help you learn more about how to better engage people on Twitter. By big names I mean people that really know how to use Twitter not necessarily nationally known figures unless they have interesting information to offer you. Here are a few ways to determine who are some big names worth following.

Ask your followers who'd they suggest following and why. Use the following sites to assist you.

www.twitter.grader.com
www.wefollow.com
www.mrtweet.com
www.twittercounter.com

TWITTER TIP- Include a good photo of yourself on your Twitter profile

One of the questions I've asked is how do you gain trust online. Without question the consistent message is by being transparent. Part of being transparent is through visual aid. Yes, having a clean, clear head shot is paramount. It makes you seem more as a real person instead of a spam bot.

TWITTER TIP- Include a short bio on your Twitter profile people read them

One of the primary ways people decide to follow you are not is by what is on your Twitter bio/profile. You only have 140 characters. Ensure that what you say is descriptive and speaks to your target audience. Keep in mind that search tools will pick up these words so it's important to use those words that truly describe you, your business and/or what you do.

TWITTER TIP- Include your official link in your Twitter profile first, then any social networks.

If you are online for business you should have your own website and a top-level domain (TLD). Having your official web address makes you look more official, people tend to take you more serious and it helps with your seo (search engine optimization). Here's a bit of a secret many people don't know. There are many Twitter Applications that will grab the data from your official Twitter Profile and put it on their site which means more links going to your official website. This helps increase your search engine ranking on sites such as Google, Yahoo and Bing. I've included some examples of top-level domain names below. Remember if Twitter, Facebook, JaWar and Youtube did it, it may make sense for you too.

jawarspeaks.com
readclickanddo.com/
makemoneyselfpublishing.com

TWITTER TIP- Give PRT love

PRT is Profile RT that's retweeting part or all of someone's Twitter profile as defined by JaWar.

The PRT invention is one of my secret weapons. Sometimes you'll notice that your Twitter Stream is quite and you'll want to strike up conversations. When you PRT 15 to 25 of your followers back to back to back, you'll get some immediate responses. This tends to work when you have at least a few hundred followers, but I recommend trying it at any level. The PRT campaign works with the Law of Karma, reciprocity, universal law and what goes around comes around.

MORE TWITTER TIPS

Below are my personal Twitter Tips you may use them in your tweets and watch as they get RT'd and bring you more followers. HOWEVER, please put RT @jawar before TWITTER TIPS, so people know you are retweeting me. It's the right thing to do.:-) Here's how your tweet will look when you RT properly.

EXAMPLE:

RT @jawar TWITTER TIP- Be yourself and change when necessary.

1. TWITTER TIPS -If you have less than 3,000 followers read 17 Twitter Tips

2. TWITTER TIP- When you engage your followers you'll gradually get more followers and the right one's too.

3. TWITTER TIP- Sometimes it's good to shut off your twitterfeed & automated API. If you add value people will miss you.

4. TWITTER TIP- Be yourself and change when necessary.

5. TWITTER TIP- #followfriday isn't an obligation that has to be reciprocated, if it is we are defeating the purpose here.

6. TWITTER TIP- Tweet 30 min a day. Engage, add value, relax!

7. TWITTER TIP- Using profanity will encourage less people to follow you, it may even get you unfollowed and blocked.

8. TWITTER TIP- Remember using ALL CAPS is like screaming and makes great messages hard to read online.

9. TWITTER TIP- When you engage your followers you'll gradually get more followers and the right one's too.

10. TWITTER TIP- Following the people that RT and RT you is good Twitter Karma and good for business.

11. TWITTER TIP- I don't pay attention to auto dms when 1) Unknown source 2) Looks like spam 3) Use of shortened url

12. TWITTER TIP- When asking a specific person to RT you for your business be prepared to invest money (marketing budget).

13. TWITTER TIP- Connecting people is generally a good idea. It helps build your personal brand.

14. TWITTER TIP- Be yourself, engage the community, add extreme value, help others make money and share happiness

15. TWITTER TIP- Be yourself people will like you or they want either way you'll have to spend the rest of your life w/ you not them

16. TWITTER TIP -When you want more followers unblock your updates.

17. TWITTER TIP- At some point your tweets should lead to emails, text, phone calls & tweetups (physical meetings)

18. TWITTER TIP- Be yourself, it takes less time than faking.

19. TWITTER TIP- Save those good RT tweets to your favorite and RT them later and frequently.

20. TWITTER TIP- Be proactive in your positive stance. Tweet words of inspiration, motivation and encouragement.

21. TWITTER TIP- If you're going to send a tweet about getting more followers have a significant number of followers.

22. TWITTER TIP- Life inspired tweets are some of the best!

23. TWITTER TIP- Putting love in your tweets is a really good idea. People tend to RT love tweets. I love that!

TWITTERRESOURCEBOOK.COM

"Using THINK, PLAN, EXECUTE will help you get more out of life."

"At the exact time you want to give up your competition keeps going."

" If your best work isn't done yet you may be on your way to greatness."

"The most prophetic words ever spoke or the most practical."

Quotes by @jawar

TWITTER RESOURCES

1. Tweetlater.com –Is the self-proclaimed productivity tools for busy tweeple (Twitter People). This is a good tool for automating a good part of your Twitter Activity.

2. Tweetube.com –According to their official website you may share pictures via email directly to tweetube, send photos from iphone or other mobile devices, share all your favorite links, bookmarks and more

3. Twtpoll.com –According to their official website Twtpoll is a feedback tool that helps you to create and distribute polls/surveys on Twitter, Facebook, FriendFeed or on any other social media site.

4. Twitterfall.com – According to their official website Twitterfall is a way of viewing the latest 'tweets' of upcoming trends and custom searches on the micro-blogging site Twitter. Updates fall from the top of the page in near-realtime.

5. Twitoria.com –According to their official website Twitoria tries to reduce Twitter's clutter by revealing friends you are following that haven't posted an update in a while.

6. Twitter-friends.com –Is another nice utility. One that makes this one is it allows you to track a conversation you're having with someone else on Twitter.

7. Twitalyzer.com – According to their official websiteTwitalyzer is a unique tool to evaluate the activity of any Twitter user and report on relative influence, signal-to-noise ratio, generosity, velocity, clout, and other useful measures of success in social media.

8. Twtvite.com – According to their official website Twtvite is an event manager tool that helps you organize Tweetups and make meaningful connections through social media.

9. Twtlong.com –According to their official website Twtlong.com allows you to share more than 140 chars text, photos, videos and maps on Twitter, Facebook, FriendFeed or on any other social media site.

10. TwtQpon.com – According to their official website TwtQpon is an online coupon creator that helps you to create and distribute coupons on Twitter, Facebook and other social media sites.

11. TwtTRIP.com – According to their official website TwtTrip is a travel organizer tool that helps you to share your travel plans, meet people and plan your next adventure on Twitter, Facebook, FriendFeed or on any other social media site.

12. Twinfluence.com – According to their official website Twinfluence is a simple tool for measuring the combined influence of twitterers and their followers, with a few social network statistics thrown in as bonus.

13. Twitseeker.com - According to their official website Twitseeker is basically an alternate search engine for finding twitter.com users - "twits" - and browsing the results all in one combined control panel.

14. Twingly.com – According to their official website Twingly is a blog search engine featuring a spam-free, faceted, social search for the global blogosphere.

15. Twitterank.com –According to their official website Twitterank calculates a score for each Twitter user indicating how engaged, interesting and/or prominent they are. As the name implies, Twitterank is sort of like Page Rank for twitter users, and uses "back references" of sorts to calculate a user's score.

16. Tweetpages.com –This site allows you to customize your Twitter background.

17. Destroytwitter.com –According to their official website DestroyTwitter is a compact though robust Twitter application built to run on Mac, Windows, and Linux using Adobe AIR. It consists of a series of canvases that constantly update to keep tweets up-to-date using notifications that appear when a new tweet arrives.

18. http://dossy.org/twitter/karma/ -This is a Twitter client that allows you to enhance your Twitter experience. Some people have found great success using Twitter Karma, perhaps you will to.

19. Tweetsmarter.com –This is another Twitter client. It allows you to add cool icons and makes rting you messages a bit easier.

20. Tweetscan.com – According to their official website they are the most complete Twitter backup available. Additionally, if you're using Twitter in business, this is a great way to export followers and to archive past successes.

21. Ifollowback.com –This site helps you determine who you should follow and vice versa.

22. Topfollowfriday.com – According to their official website if you are using twitter and #followfriday to endorse your friends TopFollowFriday.com will let you see who endorses you, and who endorses whom!

23. Nearbytweets.com – According to their official website NearbyTweets project was developed by Brian Cray to extend Twitter's capabilities into its true potential: a geography–centric social tool for networking and a business tool for building customer relationships and monitoring real–time buzz. With Nearby Tweets' sophisticated geographic layer on top of Twitter people and businesses will find Twitter more relevant, manageable, and fun!

24. Wefollow.com –According to their official website Wefollow is a Twitter Directory and search to find Twitter followers.

25. Twibes.com – According to their official website Twibes makes it easy to participate in the

conversations you care about. The more you tweet, the more you are mentioned and followed.

26. Tweetvalue.com –How much is your Twitter value worth? That's right family this site actually tells you how much your Twitter account is worth in dollars and cents. How accurate is the information? That's a good question, but it's fun to check out every now and then nonetheless.

27. Tweeght.com –This is another retweeting tool. It doesn't cost to use it and may bring you more traffic.

28. Twellow.com –According to their official website they are the Twitter Yellow Pages. It's a service of Web Pro News.

29. Localtweeps.com –According to their official website Localtweeps helps you Get found and followed by tweeps near you, Find tweeps near you based on location or keyword and Post and browse local events and specials.

30. Followwatch.com – According to their official website Followwatch is your secret detective to who's following you on Twitter. When using this service you can get hourly summaries of who you've gained or lost, get published stats and more.

31. Twitpay.me –This is a way to send and receive payment by using Twitter. You must have a Paypal Account to send payments.

32. Rt2buy.com – According to their official website Rt2buy makes it easy to sell digital content over

Twitter. All you need is a Twitpay account, a PayPal account, and something to sell.

33. Retweetsuite.com – According to their official website the Retweet Commerce Suite is a platform that individuals, non-profits, organizations, advertising agencies, public relations firms, and strategy groups can use to sell digital goods, promote brand awareness, and initiate fundraising campaigns. There are three ways to use the Retweet Suite: RT2Buy, RT2Get, and RT2Give. In order to use the Retweet Commerce Suite, you must have a Twitpay account, as well as a PayPal account.

34. Chirbit.com – According to their official website Chirbit is a free online tool for audio sharing, it enables users to record, upload, listen to and share sound bites easily and is simple, useful and fun.

35. Twitwall.com – According to their official website TwitWall is the easy-to-use, quick-to-blast-out, instant blog companion for Twitter. With TwitWall, you can embed your favorite videos and widgets, upload your photos, mp3 music or podcasts, - you name it. Just the kind of stuff to keep your followers following (fans cheering, or clients calling). All that, while still enjoying the many social-goodness and customization features you enjoy on Twitter.

36. Tweetcall.com – According to their website Tweetcall allows you to update Twitter from anywhere by speaking into a telephone by calling 1-877-Tweetcall and it's free to use.

37. Twitter.grader.com – Twitter Grader is an online tool for measuring the power, authority and reach of

a Twitter user according to their official website. They may have been one of the first tools of its' kind and is indeed one the most recognized.

38. Twhirl.org – According to their official website Twhirl is a social software desktop client, based on the Adobe AIR platform. In a nutshell Twhirl has advance features for tweeting and may make your experience there more enjoyable, productive and efficient.

39. Revtwt.com – According to their official website Revtwt gives you links to post on your Twitter account and you earn money each time someone clicks on your link. Revtwt is the self-proclaimed Twitter Advertising and Twitter Marketing Platform.

40. Tweetupbadges.com - Tweetup Badges helps you put names to faces in the offline world according to their official website.

41. Retweetfeed.com – According to their official website Retweet Feed helps discover news articles, recent events, and all kinds of other information that will actually matter to you from across the web. Retweet Feed is driven by Twitter, or more specifically, people on Twitter who choose to "retweet" or pass along interesting tweets to their own followers by preceding tweets with the letters "RT". By counting the number of times everything is retweeted on Twitter, we've found interesting news begins to emerge.

42. Twitteranalyzer.com – According to their website Twitter Analyzer is the most advanced Twitter

analytical system in the world.

43. Tweetsforacause.org – According to their official website Tweets for a Cause is an avid group of social media users who believe that friends, working in concert, can change the world. Because we believe charity begins at home, our initial effort will begin with active Atlanta tweeters, in hopes to create a mass support for local based non-profits by promoting small but organized acts of giving.

44. Twittness.com –See popular tweets in real time.

45. Geofollow.com – This is a location based directory helping you find other tweeple (Twitter People).

46. Tweepular.com – This may help you boost your Twitter popularity.

47. Tweetspinner.com – According to their official website Tweet Spinner is an enterprise-class application to help large and small businesses, and users generally, increase their Twitter productivity.

48. Klout.net/twitter/influence – According to their official website Klout measures an individual's influence on Twitter to help you understand how many of your friends are taking your recommendations for new music, movies or restaurants seriously and clicking your shared links. For businesses, Klout provides insight into who you want to be talking to about your brand and spreading the word about your product.

49. Huitter.com – This site has additional resources and tools to enhance your Twitter experience.

50. Twitterfeed.com – This site allows you to feed your blog to Twitter.

51. Retweet.it – This site helps you get more retweets.

52. Twitgoo – According to their official website Twitgoo is a quick, easy, reliable, and safe way to share images for Twitter.

53. Twitrobot.com – This is another application that helps you enhance your Twitter experience.

54. Tweetbuddy.com – According to their official website Tweetbuddy promotes and provides tools for ethical, effective management of your Twitter Followers.

55. Mrtweet.com – According to their official website Mrtweet helps you discover and maintain great relationships and find people and followers that have relevant interest.

56. Retweet.com – According to their official website Retweet is the official place to find real-time news on popular stories, images, and videos.

57. Twittermass.com – This site has tools that says it helps you find more followers.

58. Eztweets.com – According to their official website ezTweets will take your longer-than-140-characters tweets and split them in a clean way, mark the tweet in a sequential manner and post them to your

Twitter timeline all at once.

59. Twt.fm – According to their official website Twt lets you share music on Twitter.

60. Twtmob.com –According to their official website Twtmob help you get paid to tweet cool stuff to your tweeps (Twitter People).

61. Backtype.com – According to their official website BackType is a conversational search engine. We index and connect millions of conversations from blogs, social networks and other social media so you can find out what people are saying about the topics that interest you.

62. Futuretweets.com – According to their official website Futuretweets is a free service that lets you schedule your Twitter messages. Send it at a specific time in the future or send a reoccuring Tweet daily, weekly, monthly or yearly!

63. Twitreferral.com – According to their official website Twit Referral is a free service where users can enhance their Twitter profile with Pictures, PDF files, Shopping Cart, Email List Builder, plus complete contact details, web addresses and business hours.

64. Podcasttotwitter.com – This site allows you to podcast to Twitter from your telephone for free. As of this writing the service is free.

65. Twitcam.com – According to their website you can use Twitcam to stream live on Twitter. Some of the features include posting your video description and

link to Twitter for all your followers to see, chat with your viewers via Twitter right from your broadcast page and have your videos automatically archived for later viewing online.

66. Topsy.com – According to its' official website Topsy is a search engine powered by tweets.

67. Truetwit.com – This site is designed to help you determine which followers are human and which are spam bots. This could be very useful as spam runs rampant on Twitter.

68. Twiturm.com –According to their official website Twiturm is one place to store, stream and post your music to Twitter.

69. Dailyrt.com/profiles/drt-all/ - According to this DailyRT it gives the most popular tweets on the web. It's one of many tools you may use to verify the impact someone has on Twitter. At the time of this writing I appear as one of the top most retweeted persons of all time. As I continue adding value and engaging the community I will be on here when you visit the site.

70. Twitterscheduler.com – This is another application that allows you to pre-schedule your tweets. There are a number of sites that offer this application, but it's always good to have a few baskets (options). We were taught don't put all your eggs in one basket.

71. Twaitter.com – This is another Twitter application that allows you to pre-schedule tweets. While at the date of writing this I hadn't used the function I like

that there's a built in translator with this application. This is one of many apps I'm going to really look at later.

72. Tweetbots.com – According to their official website Tweetbot's lets you automate and extend your Twitter experience.

73. code-or-die.com/tweetalert/ - According to their official website TweetAlert is similar to Google Alerts. Every time your search string is being twittered, you can see this in the timeline of the registered account. Stay tuned and never miss the tweets, you're interested in.

74. Tweetbeep.com – According to their official website Tweetbeep is like Google Alerts for Twitter. Get emailed when someone is twittering about you, your company, your product, or your website!

75. Powertwitter.me – According to their official website the goal of Power Twitter is simple: make twitter better. It provides a number of features.

76. Beta.twiddeo.com – According to their official website Twiddeo is a powerful but simple service that let's you do one thing very well: Twitter updates with Video. Upload from the web, your camera phone and record from your webcam.

77. Twitvid.com – This is another application to share video on Twitter from your computer, phone or API.

78. Feedly.com – According to their official website Feedly weaves your favorite content into a fun, magazine-like start page based on Google Reader and Twitter.

79. Seesmic.com – According to their official website Seesmic is a desktop client to manage your lifestream from Facebook & multiple Twitter accounts. Create groups and searches and view them any way you like.

80. Proxifeed.com – According to their website Proxifeed creates and broadcasts automated postings into your Twitter feed. Use keywords that match your areas of interest and let Proxifeed identify relevant real-time web content. Mix-in other RSS sources too. See your feed become exciting and engaging. More and more people will notice and start following you.

81. Superchirp.com – According to their official website Superchrip is a hassle free way to charge for exclusive direct messages. Additionally, it allows you to "chirp" via direct message to people who pay to "subscribe" to you. This is actually an application I need to look into with my motivational messages.

82. Twitpub.com – According to their official website Twitpub is a marketplace made for Twitter so users can buy and sell premium tweets.

83. Twitpic.com – According to their official website Twitpic lets you share photos on Twitter. You can post pictures to TwitPic from your phone, our API, or through the site itself. I've seen a lot of people on

Twitter use this application.

84. Twitterhawk.com – According to their website Twitterhawk is real time targeted marketing engine that will find people talking on Twitter now by your chosen topic and location, allowing you to really hit your target.

85. Acamin.com – I haven't used this tool yet, but like the look of the site. It may be one to use for your own social media and Twitter activity.

86. Twiggit.org – According to their official website Twiggit is an automated service that lets your friends on Twitter know what articles you Digg.

87. Twisten.fm – According to their official website Twisten crawls Twitter for tweets about music. It then takes those tweets and throws in a play button so that you can listen to the song being talked about.

88. Twitterholic.com – According to their official website Twitterholic robots scan the Twitter public timeline for new twits to tweet. A few times a day, we calculate individual statistics for each twittering twit in our database.

89. Tweetstats.com – Get your Twitter stats including tweet per and per month, tweet timeline and reply statistics. The information is simple to read and may be helpful for those knowing how to use the data.

90. Tweetwasters.com – This is a fun site that let's you see how much time you've actually invested on Twitter so far. At the time of this writing according to Tweetwaster I had invested 35,901 total tweets

and assuming I'd spent an average of 30 seconds per tweet I would have spent 1,077,030 seconds or 17,951 minutes or 299.18 hours or 12.47 Days using Twitter. Ouch, that's a lot of time.

91. Retweetrank.com – According to their official website Retweet rank is a representative of the number of times a user have been retweeted by others recently on twitter.

92. Twitscoop.com – According to their official website Twitscoop helps you receive, send tweets and find new friends instantly, without ever reloading your page. It also helps you search and follow what's buzzing on twitter in real-time.

93. Strawpollnow.com –This is a site where you may participate in polls and/or start your own and integrate it through Twitter.

94. Monitter.com – According to the official website Monitter is a twitter monitor, it lets you "monitter" the twitter world for a set of keywords and watch what people are saying.

95. Tweetscan.com/alerts.php – According to their official website with Tweetscan you can get an email when your keywords are mentioned on Twitter and several other social media and micro-blogging sites.

96. Twitterlocal.net – According to their official website TwitterLocal is going to be purely an Adobe AIR based application that allows you to filter Tweets by location.

97. Mycleenr.com – According to their official website MyCleenr is a unique way to sort your friends by their last tweets. It allows you to get rid off all the inactive and useless accounts that you are following.

98. Followcost.com – According to their official website follow cost measures how much people tweet. We use an absolute scale (average number of tweets per day) but also measure tweets in milliscobles, or $1/1000^{th}$ of Robert Scoble's Twitter output.

99. Tweepler.com – According to their official website Tweepler is an easy, more enjoyable way of processing your New Twitter Followers. View a list of New Followers and classify them in one of two "Buckets" Follow (meaning you wish to follow them back) and Ignore (meaning you don't wish to follow them and want to archive them out of the way, reducing clutter).

100. Justtweetit.com – According to their official website Just Tweet It was created to make it easier for people using the popular micro-blogging service Twitter to find other "Tweeters" with similar interests.

101. Socialtoo.com – According to their official website SocialToo can help you be a social networking power user. Keep your follower lists in sync across networks and learn more about your relationships. Send surveys to your followers and more.

102. Twitoria.com – According to their official website Twitoria finds your friends that haven't tweeted in a long time so you can give them the boot.

103. Twitdir.com – This is a Twitter Directory, listing top 100 followed, updated and followers.

104. Whoshouldifollow.com – As its' name suggest whoshouldifollow gives you recommendations on who it thinks you'd want to follow. This is yet another application that may be fun to use and perhaps there's some business benefit as well.

105. Useqwitter.com – According to their official website Qwitter e-mails you when someone stops following you on Twitter. JaWar says when you're new to Twitter this stuff matters after while you don't really care, because you're focused on those people who you're engaged with.

106. Experttweet.com –According to their official website ExpertTweet is the fastest and easiest way to find experts on Twitter. It sounds like a cool service and it's free.

107. Twuffer.com –According to their official website Twuffer allows the Twitter user to compose a list of future tweets, and schedule their release.

108. Twibs.com – According to their official website Twibs was created by a small group of people with one purpose: Give twitter users a place to find businesses on twitter.

109. Tweetdeck.com – According to their official website TweetDeck is your personal browser for

staying in touch with what's happening now, connecting you with your contacts across Twitter, Facebook and more. TweetDeck shows you everything you want to see at once, so you can stay organised and up to date.

110. Twitterfox.net –According to their official website TwitterFox is a Firefox extension that notifies you of your friends' tweets on Twitter. This extension adds a tiny icon on the status bar which notifies you when your friends update their tweets. Also it has a small text input field to update your tweets.

111. Twitbin.com –According to their official website Twitbin is a firefox extension that allows you to keep up with all of your Twitter conversations right from your browser sidebar. Send messages, receive messages, share links, and more from Twitbin, the best twitter addon for firefox out there.

112. Tweetake.com –According to their official website Tweetake is here to allow you to back-up your followers, people you are following and Tweets with just one click.

113. Tweetbackup.com – According to their official website Tweetback is free back up for your Twitter. It runs over the Internet, gives daily backups, no installation required, easy to use and no Twitter password required.

114. Wisestamp.com – According to their official website WiseStamp Firefox extension empowers your email signature on any webmail service.

115. Hashtags.org – According to their official website hashtags are a community-driven convention for adding additional context and metadata to your tweets. They're like tags on Flickr, only added inline to your post. You create a hashtag simply by prefixing a word with a hash symbol: #hashtag, they will let you know what's happening right now on Twitter.

116. Twitxr.com – According to their official website Twitxr allows you to share pictures and status updates from your mobile.

117. Twitbuttons.com – According to their official website you may easily generate code for your twitter "follow me" button.

118. Twittergallery.com –Get a custom background, so you don't look like the millions of other Twitter Accounts.

119. Splitweet.com – According to their official website Splitweet is an easy management for multiple Twitter accounts and brand monitor. They also claim to be the definitive twitter client for heavy & corporate users.

120. Lessfriends.com – Do you want to know if the people you follow, follow you back? Lessfriends helps you find out.

121. Twitturly.com – They track what urls, people are talking about, well the most popular ones.

122. Twitterpatterns.com – Free different Twitter backgrounds.

123. Twitbacks.com – Free Twitter backgrounds.

124. Twitterbacks.com - Free Twitter backgrounds.

125. Secrettweet.com – Anonymously post your tweet to Twitter. Beware I don't know what is totally secret in life and especially online. :-)

126. Twitterfall.com – According to their official website Twitterfall is a way of viewing the latest 'tweets' of upcoming trends and custom searches on the micro-blogging site Twitter. Updates fall from the top of the page in near-realtime.

127. Twistory.net – According to their official website Twitter + history = Twistory and that's it. Add your Twitter backlog feed to your favorite calendar application and browse through your personal Twitter diary, making your Twitter history both fun and useful!

128. Tweetcube.com – According to their official website TweetCube is a 100% free file sharing service for Twitter. You can upload as many images, archives, videos and songs as you want and share them on Twitter with your followers.

129. Tweetizen.com – According to their official website Tweetizen allows you to discover tweets that matter to you. Additionally, Tweetizen is a simple web-based tool designed to help you filter the daily influx of tweets, and easily find the ones

that are relevant to you.

130. Twendz.waggeneredstrom.com – According to their official website Twendz is a Twitter mining Web application that utilizes the power of Twitter Search, highlighting conversation themes and sentiment of the tweets that talk about topics you are interested in. As the conversation changes, so does twendz by evaluating up to 70 tweets at a time. When new tweets are posted, they are dynamically updated, minute by minute.

131. Twixxer.com - According to their official website Twixxer is a photo and video sharing component for Twitter.com.

132. Tweetzi.com – This is a Twitter Search utility.

133. Status.twitter.com –This is an official Twitter page that keeps you informed on technical issues and maintenance updates with Twitter.

134. Whendidyoujointwitter.appspot.com –When did you actually start your Twitter Account? This site will tell you that. It's fun to look at as time moves on and we with it.

135. Twittieme.com – According to their official website TwittieMe is a place to advertise your Twitter page for free and get more followers. Click on "Submit your Twitter page" and once approved, your ad will appear to the right. The most recent ad is at the top and only one submission is allowed in a 24 hour time period.

136. Sitevolume.com – This app allows you to see how many times a word appears on Twitter.

137. Tweetvolume.com – This app is much like Sitevolume allowing you to see how many times a word appears on Twitter.

138. Phweet.com – According to their official website Phweet lets you accept calls with one click from your Twitter page or Twitter clients.

139. Twalala.com – According to their official website Twalala is a client for Twitter that allows you to control what you see, and more importantly, what you don't see in your twitterstream. Using Twalala, you can filter tweets out of your stream by keywords and phrases or mute individuals who get a bit too chatty. Finally, Twitter with a mute button.

140. Cotweet.com – According to their official website CoTweet is how business does Twitter. CoTweet allows multiple people to communicate through corporate Twitter accounts and stay in sync while doing so. No dropped balls, no stepping on each other's toes.

141. Twitterlap.com – This allows you to see how many followers you may have in common with someone else hence Twitterlap.

142. Addtweets.com – According to their official website Addtweets is a free service allows you to add your latest tweets to a blog or website using a small piece of JavaScript code. Enjoy!

143. Pingtwitter.com - According to their official website PingTwitter allows you to automatically update your Twitter Account when you publish a new blog post.

144. Loudtwitter.com – According to their official website LoudTwitter is the bridge that posts to your blog your daily tweets.

145. Twitiq.com – According to their official website TwitIQ is an enhanced Twitter interface that provides insight into your Twitter stream and Twitter followers.

146. Crowdstatus.com – According to their official website Crowdstatus is made up of crowds, each crowd contains people and each person in the crowd has a status. This means that you can see what everyones current status is in a crowd. Think of crowdstatus as a twitter group.

147. Twittercal.com According to their official website Twittercal is a free service that connects your Twitter account to your Google Calendar. Add events in a snap from your favorite Twitter client.

148. Twitabit.com – According to their official website Twitabit is a simple way to communicate that stays up when Twitter is down.

149. Tweet3.com – According to their official website Tweet3 is an advanced, web-based Twitter client that supports grouping, Facebook, stats, multiple accounts, pretty pictures, trending topics, and all sorts of other cool, awesome and fantastic stuff.

150. Twittertise.com – According to their official website Twittertise allows you to advertise on Twitter and track the success of branded communications with your customers. Using Twittertise you can schedule your communications on Twitter and using URL tracking technology measure the effectiveness of your traffic driving techniques on the platform.

151. Lazytweet.com – According to their official website LazyTweet is to embrace and extend the questions being asked on Twitter, progressively enhancing Twitter discussions, with the lowest friction possible, while opening those questions up to a wider audience.

152. Tweetbrain.com – According to their official website TweetBrain is a crowdsourcing service powered by the Twitter user community. It facilitates people to ask questions, get answers, and earn money from answering questions posted with a reward. It also greatly increases your reach in the Twitter community well beyond your followers.

153. Twitter.polldaddy.com – According to their official website create a poll and send it to your Twitter followers in seconds. No account necessary!

154. Twitgraph.com – Graph your Twitter activity.

155. Tffratio.com - According to their official website Your TFF Ratio (your Twitter Follower-Friend Ratio) is an indication of your Twitter popularity.

156. Easytweets.com – According to their official website Easytweets may be used to promote your

business and monitor your brands.

157. Themattinator.com – According to his official website Matt makes it easy to post to multiple Twitter accounts without having to log into each one every time.

158. Twittbot.com – According to their official website TwittBot is a service that allows multiple people to publish to a single Twitter account, and for a single person to post to multiple Twitter accounts.

159. Twittergadget.com – According to their official website TwitterGadget is a clean, robust, web 2.0 style client for Twitter.com, designed to submit and view status updates via your iGoogle homepage, Gmail account, or directly in your browser.

160. Twerpscan.com – According to their official website TwerpScan will check the number of followers of all your contacts, the number of people they are following, and then compute the ratio between those. You can easily sort the list of your contacts; display them in variable batches of 20 to 100 people; and you can follow, unfollow and/or block each contact right there on the spot.

161. Twitspam.org – According to their official website Twitspam A site dedicated to blocking social networking spammers who think that they can inundate us with their spammy messages.

162. Twithire.com – According to their official website TwitHire is a free job listing service for Twitter.

163. Twitsay.com – According to their official website Twitsay gives your Twitter account a voice.

164. Twitzap.com – According to their official website TwitZap lets you slice Twitter into channels of stuff that matters to you. Once your channels are set they will update in real-time, all in a familiar interface. TwitZap is realtime, for real. You don't have to refresh anything and talking to other TwitZap users is instant, even when Twitter is not.

165. Pwytter.com – According to their official website Pwytter is a standalone Twitter client.

166. Twitterfone.com – Use this application to send messages to Twitter using your voice.

167. Twitzu.com – An application designed to help you promote more on Twitter.

168. Feedtweeter.com – According to their official website Feedtweeter is a little service that allows you to link Twitter and Plurk to your other activities.

169. Twitrefresh.com – This site automatically refreshes your Twitter homepage.

170. Techhit.com – According to their official website you will be able to archive, manage and search your tweets the same way you manage your outlook email.

171. Twordy.com – According to their official website Twordy stems from Twitter's restriction of 140 characters per update. Twitter has a great model

with short, concise updates, but sometimes you may want to get wordy. Twordy lets you post as many characters as your heart desires. Twordy is especially useful for those Twitter conversation threads that deem more space to make your point perfectly clear. Twordy works hand-in-hand with your existing Twitter account.

172. Tweetmarks.com – According to their official website Tweetmarks adds your links to Delicious.com automatically and keeps tracks of your links on Twitter.

MOBILE APPS (applications)

1. Fring.com – Free talk, live chat and interact
2. Twitterfon.net – According to their official website is Twitterfon Simple, Clean, and Fast Twitter Client for iPhone and iPod Touch.
3. Ubertwitter.com – According to their official website ÜberTwitter for the BlackBerry line of mobile phones. We are very excited about the opportunity to provide BlackBerry users with a full featured Twitter client.
4. Tinytwitter.com – This is another Twitter Mobile Client for Blackberry's, Window's Mobile Pocket PC and Smartphone.
5. Stone.com/Twittelator – App for iphone
6. Tweetsville.com –App for iphone
7. Logpost.com – According to their official website you can post your Tweets for free using Logpost, a free Twitter client for mobile phones.
8. Itwtr.com – Twitter client for iphones.
9. Jtwitter.com – Iphone Twitter client.
10. Where.com – According to their official website Where allows you to quickly launch a mobile

experience that puts the people, places and things you look for at your fingertips while on the go.

11. Viigo.com – According to their official website Viigo is the one app you'll never want to be without.

12. Twitterride.net - Simple and Fast Twitter Client for Android.

SELF-PUBLISHING

Readclickanddo.com
Makemoneyselfpublishing.com

"My movement is loss if it is truly mine. We can do better together."

"Do you need motivation in your life? Give some to get some."

"Wickedness is like cancer, you have to cut it out."

Words by @jawar

Often, one is taught not to be a "Jack of all trades and a master of none," yet during a time of shrinking budgets and financial uncertainties, the successful business person is flexible and fluid in creating multiple opportunities.

JaWar -Motivational Speaker, Author and Business Consultant knows first hand as having overcome a severe speech impediment and being homeless. His passion for business and burning desire to help others has positioned him to start a media company, publishing business and consulting firm. He has published over 20 paperback, audio and ebooks including the Music Industry Connection Book Series and How to Self-Publish for Profit, while maintaining over 60 websites, blogs and social networking profiles.

He has managed to be effective as a music business adviser, published author, internet marketing and social media professional while consulting and delivering motivational presentations and keynote addresses for universities, businesses and foundations alike, in Atlanta, Washington D.C., Los Angeles, New Orleans, Florida, North & South Carolina, Alabama, Texas and many others.

His presentations are created to identify and share vital information in a step-by-step process necessary for success and ultimate longevity in business with aspiring entrepreneurs and those willing to demand more out of life. JaWar shows the attendee how to be a successful entrepreneur and arms them with the tools necessary to prosper in an extremely competitive business environment.

He has assembled keynote addresses, seminar series, workshops and panels that merge extremely valuable information with his own personal style to deliver easily overstood and empowering information. JaWar challenges conventional views of how to succeed in life and business by seriously exploring and promoting independence using his three step success system -THINK, PLAN, EXECUTE.

He inspires aspiring entrepreneurs to aim high, create windows of opportunity and persevere through challenging stages of a budding career. In addition, JaWar encourages networking so that those who attend the presentation may build alliances to work together toward a more prosperous future.

Furthermore, he has managed to naturally be effective as a music business adviser, published author, internet marketing and social media professional while consulting and delivering motivational presentations and keynote addresses for universities, businesses and foundations alike.

JAWAR'S SPEAKING POINTS

Think-Plan-Execute: Get What You Want Out of Life
Self-Motivation, Personal Branding and Achievement
Think-Plan-Execute: Be Happy, Healthy & Wealthy
Lead Generation in a Digital Economy
Positive Change in the Right Direction
Internet Marketing
Social Media (Twitter, Facebook, Ning, Myspace, etc.)
Creating Your Future by Acting in the Present
Creating a Positive Self-Image
Strategic Planning
Making Money Online
How to Self-Publish for Profit
The Music Business

JaWar's presentations are wrapped within his 3-Step Success System of THINK, PLAN, EXECUTE! Programs may be created to fit your specific goals and objectives.

JAWAR SPEAKING VENUES

Art Institute of Atlanta
Atlantis Music Conference
Clark Atlanta University
Emory University
Morehouse College
North Carolina Central University
Oglethorpe University
SESAC Atlanta- Tempo Tuesday
Spleman College
University of Georgia in Athens
University of Alabama
Urban Network Music Conference
YMCA

SCHEDULE JAWAR TO SPEAK

404-532-9324
www.jawarspeaks.com
jawarspeaks@yahoo.com
P.O. Box 52682, Atlanta, GA 30355

"THINK, PLAN, EXECUTE!" -JaWar

CREATING WEALTH

Whether you earn an additional $5,000 or $5,000,000 a year from the business of music, remember to always put a percentage of your earnings (money that you make) aside, preferably in a tax-sheltered account and invest your money in businesses that have nothing to do with the music industry. This is called diversification of your assets (money). In addition, you want to always pay yourself first, spend less money than you earn, carry little to no debt and keep accurate and complete records of the money you earn and spend. This will increase your chances for long-term wealth creation and retention. Educate yourself about business and money; after all if you don't mind your business and money, someone else will. To ensure you advance your own learning on saving, investing and creating wealth I have listed a few terms below that you should know.

401(k)
Annuities
Assets
Asset Allocation
Bonds
• Corporate
• Convertible
• Government
CD-Certificate Deposit
Checking Account
Compounding Interest
Debt to Income Ratio
Diversification
Dollar-Cost Averaging
Earnings
Equity
Financial Freedom
Index Funds
Inflation
Investment Portfolio

IRA-Individual
Retirement Account
Keoghs
Market Index
Money-Market Accounts
Money Market Mutual
Funds
NAV (Net Asset Value)
No-Load Mutual Funds
Passive Income
Prospectus
Real Estate
Residual Income
ROI (Return on
Investment)
Roth-IRA, SEP-IRA,
Simple-IRA
Savings Account
Stocks
Tax Sheltered Accounts
Treasury Bills

Educate yourself about investing and seek the advice of professionals who may help you verify your information. Publications that may help you become familiar with saving and investing your money are Black Enterprise, Success "What Achievers Read," The Wall Street Journal, Kiplinger, Money, Smart Money, Barron's, Investor Business Daily, Financial Times and the Money Section of USA Today. For more information on saving, investing and making your money grow; visit the following websites.

www.bankrate.com
www.blackenterprise.com
www.buyandhold.com
www.creditinfocenter.com
www.fool.com
www.indexfunds.com
www.investoreducation.org
www.jumpstartcoalition.org
www.kiplinger.com
www.marketwatch.com
www.mfea.com
www.money.com
www.moneyopolis.org
www.moringstar.com
www.rothira.com
www.smartmoney.com
www.success.com
www.tiaacref.com
www.troweprice.com
www.youdecide.com
www.vanguard.com

MAIL ORDER FORM

Please mail me the following music business items to help me achieve my goals. I have completed the attached order form and will include a money order for my total and mail it payable to:

P.O. BOX 52682, Atlanta, GA 30355, USA

Name:	
Company Name:	
Mailing address:	
City:	State: Zip:
Phone:	Fax:
Email:	
Comments:	

www.jawarspeaks.com 404-532-9324

Item Description	PRICE Per Item	# of Items	Total
How to Self-Publish for Profit:	$19.95		
Atlanta Music Industry Connection Resources for-Artists, Producers, Managers	$19.95		
Los Angeles Music Industry Connection Resources for-Artists, Producers, Managers	$19.95		
Music Industry Connection The Truth About Record Pools & Music Conferences, Talent Shows & Open-Mics Book	$19.95		
Atlanta Modeling Industry: Secrets Revealed	$19.95		
Twitter Resource Book	$19.95		
MY Music MY Business	$19.95		
SUBTOTAL	/////////		
Shipping & Handling Add $5.00			
GA residents add 7% sales tax.			
TOTAL			

"THINK, PLAN, EXECUTE!"

Thank you for making the purchase and/or reading TWITTER RESOURCE BOOK. I'm truly humbled you've allowed me to take some of your time as we can never get that back. Speaking of time I am reminded that tomorrow is promised yet we are not. When you want to get more out of this lifetime and be happy, healthy and wealthy THINK, PLAN, EXECUTE!

Please follow me @jawar and my twin @jawarspeaks. If you are new to Twitter get an account today at twitter.com. You'll also find me at facebook.com/jawarspeaks, jawarspeaks.com and at live events. ;-)

Maat-Hotep,
JaWar
404-532-9324